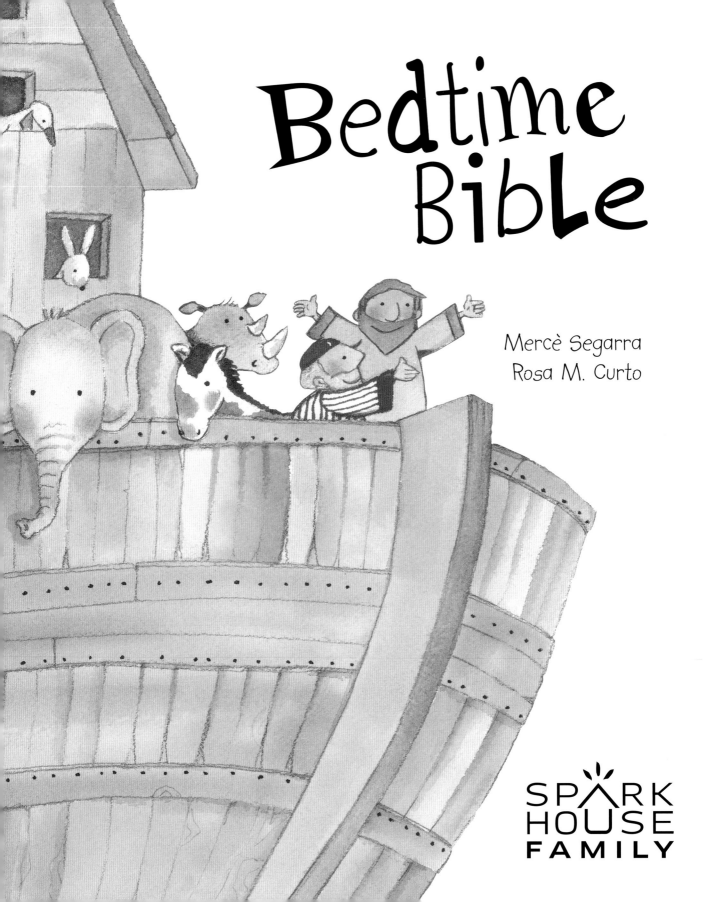

Bedtime Bible

Mercè Segarra
Rosa M. Curto

SPARK
HOUSE
FAMILY

The Old Testament

The Creation 4

Adam and Eve 6

Noah Builds an Ark 8

The Great Flood 10

Abraham and Sarah. 12

Isaac 14

Jacob's Ladder 16

Joseph 18

Joseph and His Brothers. 20

Joseph in Egypt 22

Israelites in Egypt 24

Moses. 26

The Burning Bush 28

Escape from Egypt 30

The Red Sea Parts 32

Bread from Heaven 34

The Ten Commandments 36

The Ark of the Covenant 38

The Trumpets of Jericho 40

Naomi and Ruth. 42

Samuel 44

David and Goliath 46

Solomon. 48

Daniel and the Lions 50

Jonah and the Giant Fish 52

The New Testament

The Annunciation. 54

The Birth 56

Good News. 58

The Wise Men 60

Jesus at the Temple. 62

Jesus' Baptism. 64

Jesus' Disciples 66

The Wedding at Cana 68

Thousands Fed. 70

The Parables. 72

The Lost Sheep 74

The Seed that Grows 76

The Two Houses. 78

Jesus and the Children 80

Hosanna in Jerusalem. 82

Judas Betrays Jesus 84

The Last Supper. 86

The Mount of Olives 88

The Crucifixion 90

The Resurrection 92

Jesus Ascends 94

The Old Testament

The Creation

God created the world step by step. First he made the light of day and the dark of night. Later he made the blue sky, the seas, the rivers, the mountains, the trees, and the flowers. He also made the sun that keeps us warm and the moon and the stars that shine at night. He made all animals and finally, he made people to take care of the world.

The Old Testament

Adam and Eve

Adam and Eve were the first man and the first woman God made. He offered them a wonderful place to live: the Garden of Eden. He told them they could eat fruit from all the trees except for one. But a very mean serpent told them not to listen to God, so Adam and Eve tasted the forbidden fruit. When God discovered they had disobeyed him, he was very disappointed and sent them out of the garden.

Noah Builds an Ark

After a very long time, there were more and more people on earth. Most people had forgotten God. But there was one man named Noah who remembered God. God asked him to build a very big boat called an ark. God told him he would flood the Earth and the boat would keep Noah, his family, and the animals safe.

The Old Testament

The Great Flood

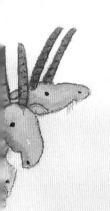

God asked Noah to board the ark with his family and two of every kind of animal. Then it rained for forty days and forty nights. Everything was covered with water, but Noah, his family, and the animals were safe. After many days, the earth was dry again and they could all come out of the ark. God made a rainbow as a promise that he would never destroy the earth again.

Abraham and Sarah

Abraham and Sarah were an old couple who had no children. One day God told Abraham to go live in a different land. Abraham trusted God and obeyed. He gathered everything he owned. Together, Abraham and Sarah started a journey to the place where God was leading them.

The Old Testament   13

Isaac

One night, Abraham heard the voice of God
telling him: "This is the land I am giving you
as a gift. It is for you and your children."

Abraham felt sad because he was old and
had no children, but God told him: "Abraham!
Look at the sky! Can you see the stars?"
Abraham nodded.

"And can you count them?" God asked him.

"Nobody can count them" answered Abraham.

Then God told him: "Abraham, one day your
descendants will be as many as the stars.
I will start by giving you a son."

God kept his promise and a year later Sarah
gave birth to a son named Isaac.

16   The Old Testament

Jacob's Ladder

*I*saac and Rebekah had twin sons, Esau and
Jacob, who were very different. When Jacob
grew up, he left home and went far away.
On his way, he stopped one evening to
sleep. He slept on a rock and had a dream.
He saw a ladder that reached the sky, with
angels climbing up and down it.

God said to Jacob: "Jacob, I will give you
a lot of land and many children. I promise
I will never leave you." Jacob trusted God
and he knew God protected him.

18　The Old Testament

Joseph

Jacob had twelve sons. One of them was named Joseph. Jacob loved him so much that he gave him a coat of many beautiful colors. The other children were jealous of Joseph because he was Jacob's favorite son.

The Old Testament

Joseph and His Brothers

One day, when Jacob's sons were tending the herds of sheep, they caught Joseph, took his coat, and sold their brother to some merchants that took him to a faraway country called Egypt.

The Old Testament

Joseph in Egypt

While Joseph was in Egypt, God protected him and gave him the power to explain the meaning of dreams. The king of Egypt had two dreams and called Joseph to help him interpret them. Both dreams meant the same thing: "Egypt will have seven years of plenty followed by seven lean years during which nothing will grow and people will go hungry." Joseph advised the king to save food during the seven years of plenty to feed the people when the bad years came.

Israelites in Egypt

Time went by in Egypt until there was another pharaoh who did not know Joseph. The new pharaoh was worried about the Israelites who lived in Egypt. The pharaoh was afraid of the Israelites and decided to make them slaves so they could not rebel against him. He also ordered all new Israelite babies born to be thrown into the river.

Moses

An Israelite mother had a baby boy and
did not want him to be thrown into
the river to drown. To protect the baby,
she made a basket made from river
plants, placed him inside, and let it float
downriver. She prayed for the basket
to reach a safe place. Fortunately, the
basket was trapped among the reeds,
where the pharaoh's daughter found
it. She decided to keep the baby and
raise him as if he were her own child.
She named him Moses, which meant
"saved from the water."

The Burning Bush

When Moses grew up, he discovered he was not an Egyptian but an Israelite. His people lived in slavery, so he decided to run away. He started a new life as a shepherd. One day he saw a burning bush. When he got close to it, he heard God's voice, saying: "Go back to Egypt and ask the pharaoh to free the Israelites." Moses obeyed the word of God and went back to Egypt, but the pharaoh refused to let the Israelites go.

The Old Testament   29

The Old Testament

Escape from Egypt

Since the pharaoh did not want to free the Israelites, God punished the Egyptian people with ten plagues. The pharaoh was very afraid and finally let the Israelites go. Moses led his people toward the Promised Land.

The Old Testament

The Red Sea Parts

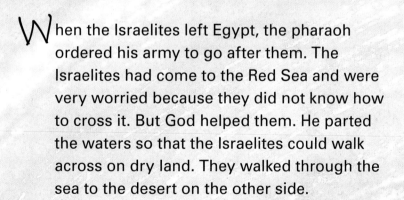

When the Israelites left Egypt, the pharaoh ordered his army to go after them. The Israelites had come to the Red Sea and were very worried because they did not know how to cross it. But God helped them. He parted the waters so that the Israelites could walk across on dry land. They walked through the sea to the desert on the other side.

The Old Testament

Bread from Heaven

The Israelites wandered in the desert and were hungry and thirsty. Moses asked God for help. God promised he would give them food and that bread would fall from the sky like rain. He gave them a kind of bread called manna. When they picked it up, they discovered it tasted like wafers made with honey.

The Ten Commandments

The Israelites came to a mountain called Sinai. One day the mountain was surrounded by a thick fog and there was thunder and lightning. God called out to Moses and gave him the laws the people of Israel had to obey. The laws were called the Ten Commandments. God wrote the laws on stone tablets and gave them to Moses for the people to read.

The Old Testament

The Ark of the Covenant

God ordered his people to make an ark, a type of chest where they could keep the stone tablets with the commandments. The Israelite soldiers kept the ark safe while they were travelling through the desert. When they stopped, they put the ark inside a tent decorated with beautiful fabric. This special tent was called a tabernacle, where they prayed and worshipped God.

The Trumpets of Jericho

After many years, Moses died and God chose a young man named Joshua as the new leader of Israel. His mission was to lead his people to Canaan. The first town they came to was Jericho, a city surrounded by very tall walls. God told Joshua to have the people walk around the city blowing the trumpets for six days. On the seventh day, when they blew the trumpets and started shouting, the walls suddenly fell down and they could go inside the city.

The Old Testament   41

42   The Old Testament

Naomi and Ruth

Naomi was an Israelite. She and her husband and two sons moved to Moab's land when food was scarce in Israel. Naomi's husband and sons died, and she was left alone with her two son's wives, Ruth and Orpah. Naomi was so sad that she decided to go back home, but Ruth did not want to abandon her, so she went with her. In Jerusalem, Ruth worked hard gathering the grain that fell to the ground in order to feed Naomi, since she loved her mother-in-law very much.

Samuel

Samuel's mother was a woman named Hannah. She wanted a son more than anything else, so she prayed and asked God to give her one. Hannah promised God that if he gave her a son, she would bring him to the temple to serve God. God gave Hannah the son she had prayed for and she fulfilled her promise. When her son was old enough, she took him to the temple and presented him to Eli the priest. And so Samuel served in the temple under the care of Eli.

David and Goliath

David was a brave young shepherd. One day he fought Goliath, a giant who everyone was afraid of. David defeated Goliath by throwing a rock from a slingshot. When he grew up, David became king, and ruled over Israel with God's help.

Solomon

When David died, his son Solomon became king of Israel. Solomon asked God to give him wisdom to rule well. God was pleased with Solomon, and gave him wisdom. All the people came to King Solomon to hear his wise advice.

The Old Testament   49

Daniel and the Lions

Daniel was a prophet. He lived in Babylon, where there was a law against praying to God. But Daniel was faithful to God. Because he was faithful, he was thrown into a den of lions. Daniel trusted God to protect him. The lions did not hurt him! In the morning, the king of Babylon realized that Daniel's God was the true God.

The Old Testament

Jonah and the Giant Fish

God asked a prophet named Jonah to go to Nineveh to tell the people to obey God. Jonah did not want to obey God, so he sailed away in a boat instead. During the trip there was a terrible storm. Jonah asked the sailors in his boat to throw him overboard. When he fell into the water, a giant fish swallowed him. Jonah prayed to God for forgiveness, and the fish spit Jonah onto dry land. Then Jonah went to Nineveh and preached to the people, just like God had told him to do.

The Annunciation

Mary lived in Nazareth. One day, an angel appeared to her and said: "You will have a son and you will name him Jesus. He will be a very special baby—the Son of God!" Mary was very excited and sang a song of praise to God.

The New Testament

The Birth of Jesus

Mary married a carpenter named Joseph. Together, they made a long journey to the town of Bethlehem. When they got there, there were so many people that all the inns were full. The only place they could find was a stable where animals lived. That night, Jesus was born, and Mary laid him down to sleep in a manger.

Good News

The night Jesus was born, shepherds were sleeping in the fields close to Bethlehem. Suddenly, a very bright light shone in the sky. An angel appeared and told them a baby had been born who would save the people from their sins. The shepherds went to visit baby Jesus in the stable.

The New Testament 59

The Wise Men

Very far away from Bethlehem, in the East, there lived
three wise men who were called "magi." One night they
saw a star shining in the sky and knew it was a sign sent
by God. They followed the star until they found Jesus.
When the wise men arrived, they worshipped the baby
and gave him gifts of gold, frankincense, and myrrh.

Jesus at the Temple

Jesus lived in Nazareth with his family. When he was 12 years old, his parents took him to Jerusalem. When it was time to go home, Mary and Joseph could not find Jesus anywhere! They looked high and low, and finally found him in the temple, talking with the teachers. The teachers were amazed at everything Jesus knew about God.

Jesus' Baptism

John the Baptist lived in the desert. He baptized people in the Jordan River. One day, Jesus came and asked to be baptized. When John baptized him, a voice from heaven said, "This is my beloved Son."

The New Testament   65

Jesus' Disciples

The time had come for Jesus to begin teaching people about God's great love for the world. Jesus needed people to help him bring his good news to the people. Jesus chose twelve helpers. Jesus called them his disciples.

The Wedding at Cana

One day Jesus and his disciples were invited to a wedding. Everyone was celebrating and having fun, but there was one problem—there was no more wine! Jesus changed six jars of water into wine, so that the celebration could continue. This was Jesus' first miracle.

Thousands Fed

Everywhere Jesus went, people wanted to meet him. One day, thousands of people came to hear Jesus speak—but there was nothing for them to eat! A boy shared his five loaves of bread and two fish. Jesus blessed the food and told his disciples to give it to the crowd. There was enough for everyone!

The New Testament   71

The New Testament

The Parables

Jesus used stories to talk about God's love. These simple stories were called parables. Each one had a lesson to help people understand how much God loved them.

The Lost Sheep

Jesus told this story: a shepherd had a hundred sheep and he lost one. The man left the other ninety-nine and went to look for his lost sheep until he found it. When he found it, he was very happy. He gathered all his friends and shared the good news with them.

The New Testament

The Seed that Grows

Jesus told another parable: a farmer plants a seed in his field. The seed stays in the ground night and day, whether the farmer is asleep or awake. Little by little the seed grows without the man knowing how. First it is just a blade of grass, then the kernels appear with the grains of wheat inside. When the kernels are dry, it is time for the harvest.

The Two Houses

Jesus said: Whoever listens to these words of mine and puts them into practice is like the wise man who built his home on solid rock. The rain fell, storms came and winds blew but the house did not tumble down because it had good foundations. But if you don't listen to what I say, then you are like a man who built his house on the sand. When the storm came, his house crumbled and fell.

Jesus and the Children

The New Testament

One day, some parents took their children to Jesus, so that he could bless them. But the disciples told them that Jesus was very busy. They sent the boys and girls away. But Jesus called them right back. He said, "Let the children come to me." He picked them up and blessed them.

The New Testament   81

Hosanna in Jerusalem

Jesus and his disciples went to Jerusalem to celebrate Passover. Jesus rode into town on a donkey. There were crowds of people everywhere. The people greeted Jesus with palm branches. "Hosanna!" the crowds cried. "Blessed is he who comes in the name of the Lord!"

Judas Betrays Jesus

The chief priests of the temple did not like Jesus. They went to Judas, one of Jesus' disciples. They paid him thirty pieces of silver to tell them where they could find Jesus.

The Last Supper

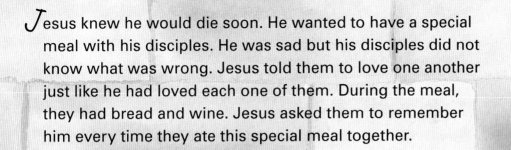

Jesus knew he would die soon. He wanted to have a special meal with his disciples. He was sad but his disciples did not know what was wrong. Jesus told them to love one another just like he had loved each one of them. During the meal, they had bread and wine. Jesus asked them to remember him every time they ate this special meal together.

The New Testament

The Mount of Olives

After supper, Jesus wanted to pray. He went to a quiet garden where he could pray in peace. Suddenly Judas appeared with the soldiers of the chief priests. They arrested Jesus and took him away.

The Crucifixion

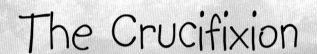

The people who had taken Jesus prisoner put him on
trial. They asked him many questions, even though
he hadn't done anything wrong. Then they brought
him to a hill and put him on a cross. Jesus died on
the cross, and all his friends were very sad.

The New Testament

The Resurrection

Jesus' friends put him in a tomb and closed the entrance with a big rock. Three days later, some women went to visit the tomb. They saw that the stone had been rolled away. Suddenly an angel appeared and told them that Jesus had risen from the dead. The women rejoiced! They left to tell the disciples that Jesus was alive.

Jesus Ascends

Jesus appeared to his friends and disciples. Jesus told them that he would send the Holy Spirit to help them spread the good news through the whole world. Then he rose up into heaven to be with God. Later, when the disciples were celebrating Pentecost, the Holy Spirit appeared to them like fire! They were filled with the power of the Holy Spirit. The disciples told everyone they met about Jesus.

The New Testament   95

Bedtime Bible

© Sparkhouse Family 2018

Published in 2018] by Sparkhouse Family in cooperation with
Gemser S.L.All rights reserved. No part of this book may be
reproduced without the written permission of the publisher.
Email copyright@1517.media.

Text: Mercè Segarra
Illustration: Rosa M. Curto
Design and layout: Estudi Guasch, S.L.

ISBN: 978-1-5064-1326-6

Printed in China